Dedicated to
Simon Rodhouse
who was tragically killed in a car crash returning from the
Great Britain v U.S.S.R. indoor match in 1983
where he represented G.B. in the shot put

Contents

Photographs

The B.A.F. acknowledges with gratitude the contribution of the late Howard Payne who provided all the sequences/photographs in this book other than: Günthör sequence – Helmar Hommel; Simon Rodhouse photograph – Mark Shearman; cover photograph of Matt Simson, Commonwealth Champion 1994 – Tony Duffy/Allsport.

About the Author

Before being appointed as a National Athletics Coach in 1981, Max Jones worked in the field of Physical Education and Recreation Management. In 1982 he took on the position of Chief Coach for Throws and in this capacity was Team Coach to the Great Britain team at European, World and Olympic Games as well as being Chief Coach for the England Commonwealth Games teams of 1986, 1990 and 1994. In 1991 he was appointed as Chief Coach for the Great Britain Junior Team.

Historical Development

Hans Woellke (Germany), the 1936 Olympic Champion, exhibits the classical side-on technique that dominated the pre-war shot scene. Woellke was the first top shot putter to benefit from systematic strength training.

Shot putting has a very ancient history. As far back as the fourteenth century Edward III prohibited shot putting by statute, fearing that the popularity of throwing might lead to a decline in archery. By the late nineteenth century the event had evolved into basically the one we know today, with the weight standardised at 16lbs (7.26kg), and the implement thrown from a 7 foot square! The event was included in the 1865 Oxford v Cambridge match and G.W. Elliot won with 9.55 metres.

Clarence Hauser (6'0"/180 lbs), by making the movement flow, reached 15.26 in 1924.

By 1928 the record had remained unbroken for 19 years, but within six years 17.40 had been reached and nine athletes had helped take the world record in stages to that distance. The man who had achieved this breakthrough was Jack Torrance (USA – 6'3"/300 lbs), who relied on his immense strength and bulk. Torrance used a high, slow hop into a powerful throwing position and relied on physical power to reach world

Fig. 1 – Ralph Rose

Fig. 2 – Jack Torrance

In 1908 the circle replaced the square and the event took on its modern form, not only in rules but also distances thrown. Ralph Rose (USA – 6'6"/235lbs) threw 15.56 in 1909, thought by many to be the ultimate record. Rose's side-on glide owed much to the man's strength and was almost a standing throw, such was the pause in the middle of the circle. The Rose technique was refined by men of lesser stature and athletes such as

record distances.

The man to supplant Torrance as world record holder was almost his direct physical opposite — athletic, light, and a superb stylist. Twenty one years old Charles Fonville (USA – 6'2"/195 lbs) threw 17.68 in 1948. He introduced a fast, non-stop, sideways glide (see Fig. 3) which was almost the ultimate in efficiency with that style of throwing.

Fig. 3 – Charles Fonville

Fig. 4 – James Fuchs

Fonville was immediately followed by James Fuchs (USA – 6'1½"/224 lbs) who attempted to add range to the shot by landing in a very deep, rear-facing position in the middle of the circle. He lost momentum, but gained in range and power and improved the record to 17.95 (1950), the last world record to be set using the side-on glide.

The man who ended his run of 88 straight wins and took the gold medal at the Helsinki 1952 Olympics was to revolutionise the event. His name was Parry O'Brien (USA – 6'3"/245 lbs). O'Brien was an outstanding High School athlete who, when only 17, threw the 12 lbs (5.44 kg) shot 17.61. He became world class using the then orthodox technique but, on a European tour in 1951, he moved further and further round at the back of the circle until eventually he turned his back on the direction of the throw.

Fig. 6 – Parry O'Brien, historically the all-time great athlete of shot putting.

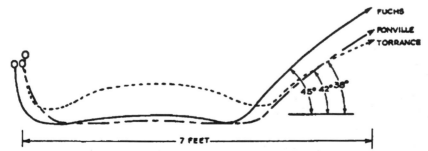

*Fig. 5 – **Path of Shot - Fuchs, Fonville, Torrance**. Note the height of Torrance's hop compared with the later record holders. Fuchs took the shot away from the neck at the back of the circle and adopted a deep lay back position in the centre from which the shot was directed to an unusual height with a 45° release angle.*

3

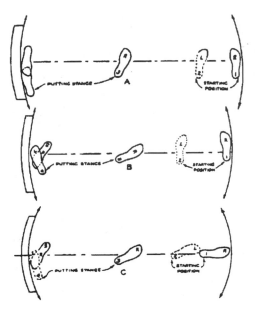

Fig. 7 – Opposite (left) are the respective foot patterns of Fonville (top), Fuchs (middle) and O'Brien (bottom). Note how similar the O'Brien and Fuchs throwing positions are, but the backward facing glide of O'Brien allowed for continuity of movement.

Nieder (USA – 20.06 in 1960) could standing put over 19 metres, in excess of the pre-O'Brien world records, such was his strength built up by weight training. The O'Brien form was accepted universally and quickly became the orthodox technique with which Nieder, Long (USA – 20.67) and finally Matson (USA – 21. 78) took the world record to previously unattainable distances.

In the late sixties the rise of the GDR as a world athletic power also brought a variation to the shot technique. Hartmut Briesenick (GDR – 21.67) spearheaded a whole wave of shot men and women who used a short glide, with a very long base (see Fig 9) in order to increase the range over which force could be applied to the implement. In the early seventies this short-long technique with a fixed feet delivery became very popular. Briesenick, Gies (GDR – 21.31) and Stahlberg (Fin. – 21.69) were successful exponents of this style, and Ilona Slupianek (GDR – 22.45) set women's world records with an extreme version of the short-long

Between 1952 and 1956 O'Brien went through 116 competitions without losing, won two gold medals and by 1959 had raised the world record to 19.30. Too much significance has been given to the technical innovation of O'Brien. In reality it added tens of centimetres, *not* metres. It was the acceptance of strength-training through barbells which coincided with the O'Brien technique that revolutionised the event. Bill

Fig. 8 – Randy Matson, who at two metres tall radically revised the record books. The only unusual aspect of Matson's technique was that he left the rear of the circle via his toes, not his heel.

Fig. 9 – Hartmut Briesenick

Fig. 10 – Al Feuerbach

Al Feuerbach (USA – 21.82) improved the world record with a superbly efficient technique,and used extreme torque at the rear of the circle to give range in the middle of the circle. Feuerbach was able to arrive in the middle of the circle with his shoulders square to the rear and his hips 90 degrees to the front. Feuerbach's version of the O'Brien technique was judged by many to be the perfect technique, and indeed Feuerbach's physique of 6'1"/240 Ibs emphasised the efficiency of his technique.

Since the early Fifties athletes had experimented with discus turns, but with little success until Aleksandr Baryshnikov (USSR) threw 20.54 in 1972 to place twelfth on the world rankings of that year.

At the same time a prodigious talent, Brian Oldfield (USA) had thrown 20.87, but had impressed observers by throwing nearly 22 metres in training at the Munich 1972 Olympics by rotating and lunging out of the circle. By 1975 Oldfield (6'4"/260 Ibs), who had turned professional, perfected his rotational shot technique *and* stayed in the limits of the seven foot circle. In May 1975 Oldfield pushed back the limits of shot putting by throwing 22.86 metres – an unofficial mark in the then amateur athletics world. Oldfield eventually regained his amateur status but lost the best years of his athletic life, although he did set an official U.S.A. record in 1984 with a 22.19 throw.

Developing almost in parallel with Oldfield was Aleksandr Baryshnikov (6'6"/ 270 lbs) who, in 1976, rotationally threw exactly 22.00 metres to become the first European to hold the world record since 1932. Baryshnikov showed that the rotational technique could be consistent by collecting medals in both the 1976 and 1980 Olympic Games. Although the rotational method of throwing has increased in popularity since the pioneering days of Oldfield and Baryshnikov, it is only in the USA where it has attracted equal numbers with that of the linear technique.

Fig. 11 – Aleksandr Baryshnikov

Fig. 12 – Brian Oldfield - rotational pioneer.

In 1976 the Olympic gold medal was surprisingly won by the twenty-one year old Udo Beyer (GDR – 6'5"/265 lbs) and subsequently, using a linear technique, he raised the world record by instalments to 22.22 metres. In 1985 his compatriot Ulf Timmermann improved the record to 22.62, only for Beyer to regain it in 1986 with 22.64. In 1987 Alessandro Andrei (Italy 6'2"/260 lbs) approached 23 metres with a new record of 22.91. It was left to Timmermann to break the 23 metre barrier in 1988 with a throw of 23.06 metres in Greece.

Randy Barnes (USA – 6'5"/280 lbs) gained a silver medal behind Timmermann in the 1988 Olympic Games and two years later threw rotationally over 23 metres twice within six days (23.12 and 23.10) but was subsequently banned for steroid abuse, although the records will remain.

It is interesting to note that rotational throwers are a rarity in women's shot putting, probably due to the event being dominated by the former 'Eastern Bloc' throwers. Three women have exceeded 22 metres with the 4 kg shot, the aforementioned Slupianek (GDR 5'11"/220 lbs), Helena Fibingerova (Czech) and Natalya Lisovskaya (Rus.) with the latter throwing 22.63 in 1987.

THE BARRIER BREAKERS

16.04	Emil Hirschfeld	(GER)	1928	16 metres	16.20	Galina Zybina	(USSR)	1953
17.40	Jack Torrance	(USA)	1934	17 metres	17.25	Tamara Press	(USSR)	1959
18.00	Parry O'Brien	(USA)	1953	18 metres	18.55	Tamara Press	(USSR)	1962
18.42	Parry O'Brien	(USA)	1954	60 feet (18.29m)		as above		
19.06	Parry O'Brien	(USA)	1956	19 metres	19.07	Margitta Gummel	(GDR)	1968
20.06	Bill Nieder	(USA)	1960	20 metres	20.09	Nadyezhda Chizhova	(USSR)	1969
21.52	Randy Matson	(USA)	1965	21 metres	21.03	Nadyezhda Chizhova	(USSR)	1969
	as above			70 feet (21.33m)				
22.00	Alex Baryshnikov	(USSR)	1976	22 metres	22.32	Helena Fibingerova	(CZE)	1977
23.06	Ulf Timmermann	(GDR)	1988	23 metres				

N.B. Brian Oldfield (USA), as a professional, exceeded 22 metres several times in 1975 with a season's best of 22.86 metres.

BRITISH SHOT DEVELOPMENT

Judy Oakes – Commonwealth gold medallist and Britain's first 19 metre shot putter.

Geoff Capes – Britain's greatest ever shot putter – a former world number one (1975) who still holds the British record for the event 21.68.

The early history of British shot putting was dominated by Dennis Horgan, who in 1904 set a world record of 14.88 metres from a seven foot square and collected 13 AAA titles. Since Horgan hailed from Ireland, it can be said with some justification that the first British athlete to approach world standards was John Savidge (6'7"/240 lbs); he broke Horgan's old record in 1949, increased it dramatically in several increments to 16.83 metres in May 1954 and ranked twelfth in the world rankings.

The first British athlete to break into world class was Arthur Rowe (6'1"/240 lbs) who, after a late introduction to the event, improved dramatically to win the 1958 European Championships exhibiting superb technique. Despite failing at the Rome Olympics (1960), he went on to threaten the world record with 19.62 metres before turning to professional rugby league.

Rowe was followed a decade later by a young man of immense physique (6'5½"/300 lbs) and strength, Geoff Capes. Capes dominated British shot putting for a decade, taking the record up to 21.68 metres in 1980, along the way winning the European Indoor Championship and merit ranking first in the world in 1975.

The first woman shot putter of international standing was Suzanne Allday, who in eleven increments raised the British record from 12.70 metres (1953) to 15.18 metres (1964). Pentathlete Mary Peters brought athleticism to the event and raised the record to 16.31 metres in 1966. In 1980 Angela Littlewood broke the record in the qualifying pools of the Olympic Games when she threw 17.53 metres. Judy Oakes took over the event and totally dominated in the nineteen eighties, raising the record to 19.36 metres, and was joined by Myrtle Augee in 1990.

BARRIER BREAKERS

15.66	John Savidge	1949	15metres		15.18	Suzanne Allday	1964
16.58	John Savidge	1951	16 metres		16.31	Mary Peters	1966
17.30	Arthur Rowe	1958	17 metres		17.17	Angela Littlewood	1980
18.59	Arthur Rowe	1959	18 metres		18.06	Meg Ritchie	1983
19.11	Arthur Rowe	1960	19 metres		19.00	Judy Oakes	1986
20.18	Geoff Capes	1972	20 metres				
21.00	Geoff Capes	1974	21 metres				

Basic Mechanics of the Shot Put

Maggie Lynes demonstrates an ideal angle of release.

It is important that the coach shall have at least a working knowledge of the mechanical principles appertaining to the event. Such knowledge will ensure that a novice will be taught a technique based on sound principles; then later the athlete's own style can be developed.

The coach should always allow for the fact that the athlete is a human being and not a machine. The laws which govern the performance of machines cannot be so easily employed to explain the actions of the shot putter, since the human frame is infinitely more complex than any machine.

The distance which the shot will travel, however, does undoubtedly depend upon three fundamental factors:

(A) its height of release
(B) its angle of release
(C) its speed of release.

Factors affecting distance in shot putting

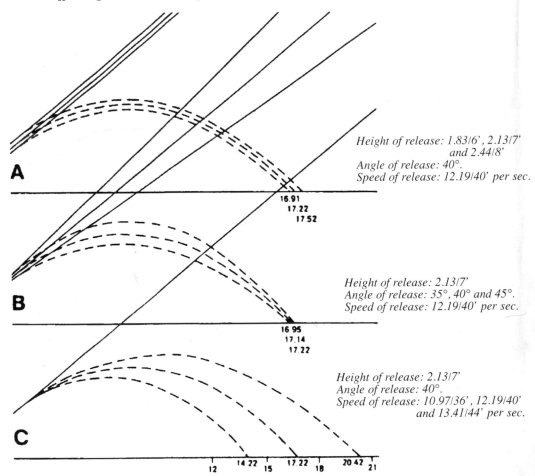

A

Height of release: 1.83/6', 2.13/7'
and 2.44/8'
Angle of release: 40°.
Speed of release: 12.19/40' per sec.

16.91
17.22
17.52

B

Height of release: 2.13/7'
Angle of release: 35°, 40° and 45°.
Speed of release: 12.19/40' per sec.

16.95
17.14
17.22

C

Height of release: 2.13/7'
Angle of release: 40°.
Speed of release: 10.97/36', 12.19/40'
and 13.41/44' per sec.

12   14.22   15   17.22   18   20.42   21

Above graphs by Jack Sweeney from article 'Fundamentals of Throwing' – 'The Circle' magazine (June 1978)

Release Speed

As can be seen from Jack Sweeney's graphs, RELEASE SPEED is the most important. A small percentage increase in release speed will always bring about a greater percentage increase in distance if all other factors remain unchanged. A 10% increase in release speed will bring about a 21% increase in distance *(Tom Ecker – Track & Field Technique Through Dynamics)*. The coach should therefore be constantly looking at ways of increasing release speed. The release speed is a function of the total effective force which the thrower is able to bring to bear upon the shot before free flight is attained.

Angle of Release

The optimum angle of release for the projection of a missile for distance is 45 degrees, but this assumes that the point of landing is on the same level as that of the release. Obviously a shot putter releases the shot at 1.90-2.30 metres above ground level and therefore the theoretical optimum release angle is 40 to 42 degrees. Coaches should not be too mathematical since correct technique will result in the optimum angle of release. The further the distance thrown, the closer the angle of release will be to the optimum – a 9 metre put will have a release angle of 38 degrees 20 whereas a 20 metre put will have 41 degrees 60. A thrower who releases at less than the optimum angle for his distance cannot increase it by altering the arm movement since his speed across the circle and the vertical lift by his legs/back muscles have effectively determined the angle of release.

Height of Release

Compared to the speed of release, the height at which the implement is released has a comparatively small effect upon distance – but since competitions may be won by a single centimetre, the coach must ensure that the maximum release height is attained. A sound technical model will ensure optimum release height; a low release height in relation to the athlete's stature is a symptom of poor technique.

Work

WORK = FORCE x DISTANCE

A world class thrower will exert his strength and speed (FORCE) over as great a range as possible (DISTANCE) in order to achieve a good throw (WORK). He must ensure that his force is applied for the longest period possible and therefore:

FORCE x TIME = IMPULSE

The coach devotes his time to creating a rangey technique (TIME) and the thrower spends hours conditioning himself with barbells in order to increase the FORCE part of the equation. The IMPULSE can be increased (1) by lengthening the TIME for which the FORCE is exerted, or (2) by applying a larger FORCE for the same amount of TIME.

Obviously, from the above formulae, the longest possible acceleration route should be employed, but the coach should always take into consideration the athlete's mobility and strength. The range should be that through which the athlete can reach maximum release speed, which is not always the greatest range.

Summation of Forces

The larger muscles of the body are heavier and best suited to moving heavy loading relatively slowly. The smaller muscles are therefore better used moving lighter loadings at great speed. In throwing there is always a definite sequence of muscle action, using the large muscles such as the legs and trunk first and using the arm 'fast and last'. The sequence is legs – trunk – arm. The summation of forces – slow to fast – legs first, arm last and fast – should form the basis of early coaching.

Ground Reaction

To achieve maximum speed of release, contact must be maintained with the ground for as long as the athlete is in contact with the implement, so that the counter-thrust of the ground enables him to impart his force. Certainly a thrower can exert his greatest force when both feet are in contact with the ground. The novice should be developed using contact with the ground during the final throwing movement.

Many world class men however can be observed to lose contact before the shot has left the hand. This will have a negative effect in that the reaction that had previously been provided by the ground must now be absorbed by the athlete's body, pushing him backwards and therefore losing range. Then why do so many throwers fail to keep contact? This question can be answered by the following considerations:

(i)   Athletes with a large mass absorb the reaction, and its effect is thus minimised

and

(ii) The loss of contact with the ground before release is caused by the explosive power of the vertical lift by the legs. The small reduction in thrust is acceptable because it is more than compensated for by the acceleration of the shot caused by this powerful vertical lift.

Hinge Moment

When the athlete makes ground contact with the left leg at the front of the circle, there is a braking effect which causes forward rotation. In the Hinge Moment all parts of the thrower's body above the centre of gravity are speeded up. This would certainly be true if the body were rigid, but unfortunately it is not and therefore the benefits are much less than was once assumed (Fig. 13).

Fig. 13 – Hinge moment in the vertical plane.

This principle also applies to the transverse plane, but on a much smaller scale due to the radius being small when compared with that in the vertical plane (Fig. 14)

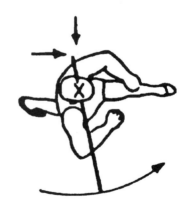

Fig. 14 – Hinge moment in the transverse plane.

The Rules

The Implements

The shot shall be made of solid iron, brass or any metal not softer than brass. It may be constructed from a shell of such metal and filled with lead or other similar material. It must be spherical in shape and the surface shall have no roughness and the finish shall be smooth. The shot shall weigh 7.26kg (16 lbs) for men and 4 kg for women. For younger throwers the competition weights are as follows:-

MEN	U-20	U-17	U-15	U-13
	6.25kg	5 kg	4 kg	3.25 kg
WOMEN		U-17	U-15	U-13
		4 kg	3.25kg	2.72 kg

N.B. For all BAF Junior (17-20) competitions it is recommended that the 6.25 kg implement be used, except for the area and national championships when the senior (7.26 kg) shot will be used.

The Circle

The circle shall have an inside diameter of 2.135 m/7 ft. It may be marked by a painted white line, 7.5 cm wide, although the use of a metal band 6mm thick, sunk flush into the ground into which it is set, is to be preferred. Where possible the surface of the circle should be of concrete, trowelled flat, so that the sand comes through to the top to give it a rough finish like sandstone. This surface should be 2 cms lower than the top of the rim. Where possible a strip of concrete should be laid outside the rim and trowelled level with it in order to prevent its distortion during use. The recommended depth of the metal band and of the concrete strip is 75 mm approx. The rear half of the circle should be indicated by a white line 5 cm wide extended outside the circle for at least 75 cms on either side, the theoretical extension of this line across the circle dividing it into front and rear halves with the rear edge passing through the centre of the circle.

The Stopboard

The stopboard shall be made of wood and be placed at the front of the circle between the lines of the radii forming the sides of the landing area. It should therefore be slightly curved and measure 1.21 - 1.23 m long by 11.2 - 11.4 cms deep. It should be firmly fixed into the ground so that its inner edge coincides with the inner edge of the circle, and it should be painted white.

Fig. 15

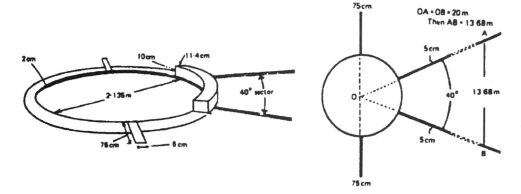

13

The Landing Area

For a valid put the shot must fall completely within the inner edges of lines marking a sector of 40 degrees set out on the ground so that the radii cross at the centre of the circle.

The Put

(a) The throw shall be made from within the circle.

(b) The throw must commence from a stationary position within the circle.

(c) The shot shall be PUT from the shoulder with one hand only.

(d The shot must not be brought behind the line of the shoulders.

(e) The competitor is allowed to touch the inside of the rim or stopboard.

(f) Competitors must not spray or spread any substance on the surface of a throwing circle nor on their shoes.

(g) It shall be a foul throw and not allowed to count in the competition if the competitor, after stepping into the circle and commencing to make a throw:

    (i) touches either the top of the stopboard or circle or the ground outside with any part of the body

or

    (ii) fails to keep the shot touching, or in close proximity to, the chin, or permits the hand to drop below this position during the action of putting.

(h) The competitor is allowed to interrupt a trial once he has started it, to put the shot on the ground and to leave the circle, if he wishes, before returning and adopting a stationary position again and re-starting the trial. He may even thus interrupt a trial more than once provided that he completes it within the maximum time allowed which is normally 1½ minutes.

(i) The competitor must not leave the circle until the shot has touched the ground and shall then, from a standing position, step out of the circle from the rear half.

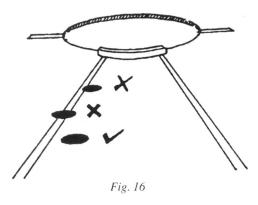

Fig. 16

The Competition

The competition may be decided in one of the following ways:

(a) By allowing each competitor from three to six throws.

(b) By allowing each competitor three throws, after which the best three to eight competitors are given three further throws.

(c) By holding a special qualifying competition before the competition proper, in which the putters are permitted three throws in which to achieve a pre-arranged qualifying distance. In this way entry is gained to the competition proper which may be conducted via methods (a) or (b) above.

Competitions are very rarely limited to three throws, and six (or three plus three) are more usual. In all cases, the competition is decided on the best of each competitor's trials throughout, with the exception only of those efforts made in a qualifying competition, as in method (c). In the event of a tie, the next best efforts of the tying throwers are compared. If this does not resolve the tie, then the third best are compared, and so on. In the unlikely event of a tie still remaining for first place after all six throws have been used the competitors must put again until the tie is resolved. For positions other than first place in these unlikely circumstances a tie would be given.

SAFETY IN THROWING

Throwing is a perfectly safe pastime that can prove lethal if simple common sense rules are not followed by the coach and the athlete. The following rules should always be adhered to.

(1) Throwing implements should at all times be treated with respect. They should not be played with or mishandled, especially when being carried from the equipment store to the track.

(2) When throwing in a group situation the golden rule 'ALL THROW THEN ALL RETRIEVE' should be strictly adhered to. It is also essential that the implements be carried back to the circle and NEVER thrown or rolled back.

(3) The sector or area into which the shots are thrown should be marked in some way since athletes/bystanders may be unaware of your intentions.

(4) The thrower should always ensure that there is no one in the landing area or probable line of flight of the implement before the throw is made. The thrower should be aware of his/her responsibility.

(5) Always inspect the throwing circle to ensure that it is safe to throw from - a loose stop board or muddy circle can cause personal injury or a misdirected throw.

(6) Wet implements increase the chance of accidents and extra vigilance should be exercised in such conditions.

(7) The shot event is a dynamic movement with a heavy implement and it is unsafe to practise without having first warmed up, thus making the risk of physical injury, eg pulled muscle, considerably less.

Natalya Lisovskaya (RUS) – World record holder and former Olympic Champion.

Techniques of Shot Putting

The following pages are devoted to a detailed analysis of shot putting with the aid of sequence photographs. While sequence analysis is useful, it does not convey the feel, rhythm or continuity of shot putting. A photograph represents one point in time and does not show what happened immediately afterwards. No sequence conveys what the athlete was intending to do or the concept he was working to. The coach must spend many hours standing at the circle, observing throwers, in order to gain expertise in shot putting. Articles, descriptions, analysis - these are all useful, but are only part of the learning process .

In the following technical descriptions right-handed technique has been described. Left handed athletes/coaches should substitute right for left and vice versa. In the majority of the text athletes are described as male - no slight is intended against the female exponents of the art of shot putting.

Fig. 17

THE GRIP

The shot should be placed at the base of the middle three fingers with the little finger and thumb supporting the shot held clear of the palm. The fingers should not be stretched apart. The most commonly used carry is to press the shot into the hollow at the base of the neck.

Individuals are advised to experiment with both the grip and the carry position as this aspect of technique has many variations and preferences. Rotational throwers should carry the elbow high and have the palm facing upwards.

Former British 20 metre shot putter Mike Winch shows the correct positioning of the shot during the putting movement.

KEYS TO GOOD THROWING

Before taking a detailed look at the event, it is worth considering its basic fundamentals which account for the vast majority of the distance achieved.

L1

L2

L3

L4

L5

Balance

No matter how strong and explosive an athlete is, he will not be able to express this force if he is unbalanced. Balance must be achieved at the back of the circle since, once lost, it is unlikely that it can be recovered later in the throw.

Acceleration

The thrower must aim to go from SLOW to FAST – starting the throw slow, finishing it fast. The acceleration actually achieved is not totally linear.

Rhythm

Linked with the concept of slow to fast is the rhythm of the event. Start smooth, finish fast with a controlled acceleration into the power position, a slight subsidence of overall speed, then a rapid acceleration during the putting action. This rhythm comes with practice and must be felt if success is to be achieved.

Legs Dominant

The throw is dominated and dictated by the legs. The legs/feet dictate the speed, rhythm and timing of the throw and provide the majority of the impulse. If the legs are right, it will almost certainly follow that the whole throw will be right.

Range

The thrower's force must be applied over as great a range as possible, taking into consideration the athlete's strength and mobility. To work over as long a range as possible the athlete should move from LOW (back of circle) to HIGH (at release).

L6

L7

L8

Left Side Brace

The final throwing action must be performed against an erect, braced left side, so that the right side of the body can work against it. This 'blocking' of the left side will be a pre-requisite to an explosive finish.

L9

Sequence: Natalya Lisovskaya (RUS) – World Champion 1987, Olympic Champion 1988

Relaxation

The athlete must aim to relax during phases of the throw from which explosive movement can effectively develop. Long throws cannot be forced.

L10

Werner Günthör (Switzerland) – World Champion 1987, 1991, and 1993

LINEAR SHOT TECHNIQUE

Glide or Shift

AIM – *to give the shot initial momentum and arrive in the centre of the circle at optimum speed and in a balanced position.*

Once having taken up his preliminary stance, the athlete has a choice of several methods of obtaining the pre-glide starting position. The classical 'T' position pioneered by Parry O'Brien in the early 1950's enabled athletes to extend the shot beyond the back rim of the circle (Fig 18). It was assumed that any increase in range would add to the velocity of the shot, but it is range in the power position that is today considered of paramount importance since this is where great increases in velocity occur (Fig 22). The classical 'T' method is itself a gymnastic feat and often results in an unbalanced starting position. The modified 'T' position is used by the majority of throwers and gives rhythm and movement to the start of the glide. For those who have balance problems at the back of the circle, the two-footed start will provide a stable initial movement and perhaps give the athlete a greater feeling of security.

In the photo sequence (next pages) Günthör has moved through a modified 'T' position before dropping down into a relaxed balanced starting position (G1), hips/shoulders square to the rear and shot to the right of the knee.

From this balanced position, the thrower allows his centre of gravity to fall under control (G2) towards the front of the circle. When this fall occurs, the centre of gravity is in a favourable position for moving in the direction of the stopboard. The right leg will then initiate a vigorous drive applying pressure against the ground, whilst the left leg is pushed smoothly, but quickly, towards the stopboard (G3). The thrower must use the right leg as the propelling force, not the left leg which performs a smooth fast low movement to the front of the circle (G4-5). The thrower should ensure that contact is broken at the back of the circle by the heel (G6). It is a mistake to leave 'toe last', since this method is less efficient and would normally cause the torso to rise during the glide. The glide must be made by the legs only, and not be assisted by movements of either the torso or the free arm. The non-throwing arm should be relaxed and passive and this may be helped by turning the palm of the hand outwards (thumb down). Shoulders should face the rear and the athlete's eyes should be focused on a point to the rear of the circle. The thrower should aim to keep low with the shot placed to the right of the driving leg (G1-8). How low and 'closed' the athlete is depends upon the strength of the athlete; novice throwers will

Fig. 18

(a) Classical 'T'   (b) Modified 'T'   (c) Two-footed start

start higher, and be higher in the power position.

During the early phase of the glide the right foot/knee/hip should rotate inwards (G8) to ensure that an active throwing position is attained.

KEY POINTS

BALANCE
RIGHT LEG DRIVE
LEFT LEG FAST AND LOW
SHALLOW LOW HOP

MID GLIDE

The athlete should break contact with the ground and aim to perform a low, shallow hip/glide (G8). Athletes who drag/scrape their rear leg along the floor often have problems in reaching an effective power position. It is far better to use a low hopping movement with the foot barely touching the circle surface and be able to place the rear leg in an effective power position. Using an effective hop, the athlete can also benefit from a small stretch reflex when the rear leg lands in the centre of the circle.

Many throwers strive to keep the shoulders square during this phase by forcing the left shoulder to stay low. This can cause shoulder tension, and therefore a slight raising of the left shoulder can be permitted during the glide. The left arm should remain long, relaxed and to the rear. At the back of the circle, the combined forces created by the left leg extending and the right foot exerting force against the ground begin to produce a counter clockwise rotation of the pelvis, which will continue when the right foot leaves the ground. This should help the turning of the right hip and leg to ensure an active power position.

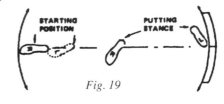

Fig. 19

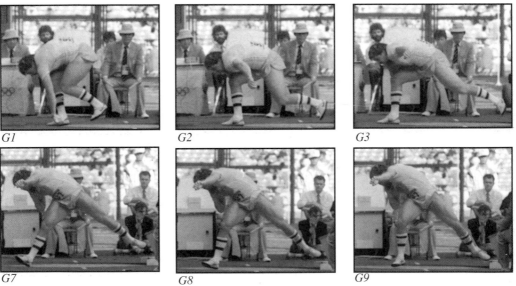

G1   G2   G3

G7   G8   G9

KEY POINTS

LOW SHALLOW GLIDE
SHOULDERS CLOSED
HIPS OPENING

POWER POSITION

AIM – *to achieve a balanced, rangey position with optimum speed.*

The effectiveness of the power position is judged when both feet are grounded (G11), and not before. The right foot during the glide should have turned to land at between 10 o'clock and 11 o'clock (Fig 20) with the hips in an open position. Some throwers, such as former world record holder Al Feuerbach, can achieve 9 o'clock, but care must be taken not to sacrifice range to achieve such a foot/hip position. Such turning of the foot aids both torque and subsequent speed of hip strike. The left

leg should ground close to the stopboard, partially open (G11-12) and pointing in the direction of the throw (7 o'clock). As seen in Fig 19, the left foot should be slightly off centre with the left toe directly in line with the right heel or better still the right instep. This off-setting allows the hip to be driven through without restriction. If the left foot is too much off centre (bucketed) then the thrower will find it difficult to execute a blocking movement or even be unbalanced. If the thrower allows the front foot to drift to his right it will block the delivery and an effective hip drive will be difficult to execute.

Fig. 20

'Clock' orientation of the shot put

G4   G5   G6

G10   G11   G12

23

The power position adopted should be a rangey one with the shot held back both horizontally and transversally, with the eyes still firmly focused to the rear and the plane of the shoulders square to the rear (G11). The novice athlete should think of chin-knee-toe being the line (looking from side on) and allow the shoulders to have become slightly open (Fig 21a).

More advanced throwers will have this chin-knee-toe line inclined (60°-70°) (Fig 21b) more towards the rear. With the elite throwers the chin-knee-toe concept will not hold true if viewed from the rear (Fig 21c) since the athlete will try to keep the shot to the right of the near knee. The depth and the range of the power position will depend upon the strength and mobility of the athlete.

Fig. 21c

Almost all athletes will unconsciously allow the shot to drift forward (G10-11) before any explosive lift is made with the legs. Perhaps this drifting is essential since leg muscles cannot pull the shot, only push it, and therefore the shot must be over the right foot before the final throwing movement commences. This drifting is perhaps better left uncoached since the correct timing will develop with time and practice.

Fig. 21a	*Fig. 21b*

KEY POINTS

CHIN-KNEE-TOE
OPEN HIPS
CLOSED SHOULDERS

Mike Winch exhibits an inclined chin-knee-toe line in the power position.

24

THE THROWING ACTION

AIM – *to apply force to the shot over as great a range as possible.*

Looking at photographs G11 through to G18 the following points can be observed:

(a) The legs/hips lead the shoulders/shot throughout the movement.

(b) The work of the legs is initially horizontal (G11-13) and later vertical (G14-18).

(c) The left side of the body is held rigid (blocked) (G15-17) to allow the right side of the body to work effectively.

(d) The arm is used very late (G17) and very fast.

The right leg action is the key element. The hips are pushed through ahead of the shoulders, which in turn produces torque which assists the final strike. The action of the right leg must be both long and quick – keep it working for as long as possible. The action of the left leg is to remain soft initially (G13-15) maintaining a slight bend and 'give' with the horizontal movement. When the hips are square to the front, the left leg strikes (G16-17) with the putting arm to give the shot vertical lift. The action of the legs could be broadly summarised as being initially to rotate and then to lift.

The thrower must ensure that he delays the rotation of the shoulders and that the elbow of the throwing arm is kept high (G15) throughout the movement. The function of the arm is to add more speed to an already fast moving implement, the arm being a relatively weak part of the body but a very fast moving one. If the arm is used too early, it will lose its effectiveness – the old adage 'arm fast and last' is a good one

It is of paramount importance that the left side is blocked/braced (G15-18), so enabling the final thrust of the right side of the body to be both powerful and effective. The left arm should not be allowed to sweep too far backwards, but rather be stopped (blocked) suddenly to aid and add to the strike of the putting arm.

G13 G14 G15

G16 G17 G18

The athlete should feel that he is chasing the shot out of the circle and the arm and shoulder should 'punch' the shot away (G18-19-20) releasing the implement as high as possible. Some athletes (a minority) will lose contact before the shot is released due to a powerful, explosive, vertical lift of the legs from a comparatively short base. Although this is mechanically inefficient (action + reaction), to eradicate this would mean that the full power of the legs could not be used. A significant minority of world class male shot putters release off the ground, but this should not be taught or even encouraged since it is perhaps a necessary evil of having immensely powerful legs. Having the left foot down at the moment of release applies to 99% of shot putters and should be taught as the basic technical model.

The angle of release is around 35°-42° and is a natural consequence of correct technique. A poor angle of release is a symptom, not a cause.

KEY POINTS

LEGS ROTATE, THEN LIFT
LEFT SIDE BRACE
ARM FAST AND LAST

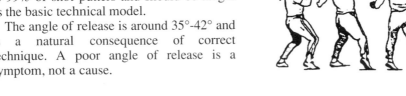

G19 G20 G21

G22 G23

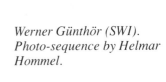

Werner Günthör (SWI). Photo-sequence by Helmar Hommel.

REVERSE

AIM – *to stay in the circle without inhibiting the throwing action*

The reverse starts immediately after the final delivery, during which the athlete has followed the shot beyond the circle, and not before the shot has left the hand. The reverse should be the result of the throwing action and not part of it.

More often than not the revese is a natural reaction to the athlete, but if it is found to be difficult the athlete should be instructed to lower his centre of gravity. This will aid recovery since, if he stands tall after the throw, he is more likely to foul. An effective blocking action during the throwing action will assist in staying in the circle. Novice athletes should have little need actively to reverse and a *fixed feet* throw should be taught.

KEY POINTS

> REVERSE AFTER THE THROW
> LOWER CENTRE OF GRAVITY

Analysis of Günthör's Technique

Fig. 22

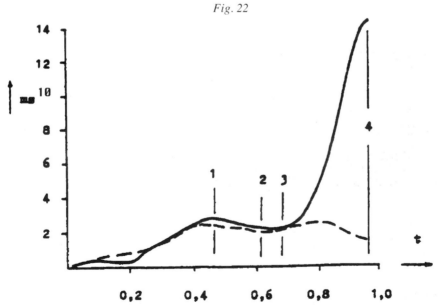

W. Günthör: 22.23m. Velocity of implement and centre of gravity movement (SUSANKA/STEPANEK 1988)

1 – *rear leg leaving back of circle*
2 – *planting rear leg - - - path of centre of gravity*
3 – *planting front leg - - - velocity of implement*
4 – *release*

Fig. 23

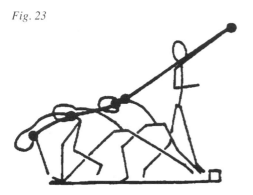

W. Günthör: distance 22.23m. Implement position at the start of the glide, planting front leg release.

Fig. 24

Sequential analysis of Günthör's put.

Helma Knorscheidt (21.19 in 1984) exhibits the classical GDR short-long style of linear throwing.

LINEAR VARIATIONS

(a) Short-long technique

This is a variation made popular by the G.D.R. putters of the late Sixties e.g. Hartmut Briesenick, and consists of a short glide and a long throwing base (Fig. 15). The thrower lands with his right foot in the rear half of the circle pointing at 11 o'clock, and then drifts sideways and hits the shot forward and upward. Due to the long base, delivery is made over a fixed front foot. Advocates of this technique argue that the long base gives the athlete great range over which to apply force. But even the strongest athletes can never get over the left leg and tend to lose range at the front. Moreover, the left leg can only strike back and not up due to this factor. Tall, rangey throwers with great strength are necessary for this technique.

(b) Fixed feet delivery (Fig. 26)

This is very similar to the orthodox linear throwing except that both feet are kept down during the final throw. It is quite extensively used by female throwers and gives solid, consistent performances. (More elite men performers find it difficult to keep grounded due to tremendously powerful leg muscles.) It is an excellent method for

Fig.25

novices, since it makes the technique simple and stable and ensures that both legs are used during the throw.

Fig. 26

(c) *Linear two-leg lift (Fig. 27)*
Here the athlete glides to a narrow base, leaving the shot well back. The athlete then drifts sideways until the centre of gravity is between the feet, and then exerts a two-legged vertical lift. This variation needs good timing, but the benefits of using both legs are great.

Fig. 27

DRILLS

Breaking the whole skill down into part skills is a well-established method of

improving technique. The number of drills that can be used to develop shot technique are numerous, and those described below are only a few of those that can be utilised.

Linear

Fixed feet drills
An integral part of the skill development of any thrower from novice through to Olympian. The athlete performs a standing throw but keeps both feet fixed, only allowing them to turn with the throw, not move forward. This stabilises the technique and allows the athlete to feel the legs working – the most important factor in successful shot putting. It is also beneficial to perform fixed feet throwing with a glide.

Partial Standing Throws
These are performed to develop technique

Fig. 28a

Fig. 28b

aspects at the end of the putting movement, such as the left side block and the co-ordination of the left leg and putting arm strike. The athlete commences the movement with the weight over the rear leg and in a position just before the putting arm would be used. The rear leg pushes the bodyweight forward, but its minimal role in this drill allows the athlete to concentrate upon the front leg and putting arm. This is normally difficult in a full putting movement, due to the dominance of the explosive rear leg movement.

Kneeling Standing Throws (Schwarbeck's Exercise)

An excellent drill to develop strength in the rear leg, and also to make the athlete feel the importance of the rear leg/hip movement.

Fig. 29b

Fig. 29a

Stop Check Drill

Here the athlete glides, then stops in the power position to check correct feet alignment, position of the shot etc. After a pause the throw is completed with a fixed feet put.

Fig. 29c

COMPARISON OF TWO WORLD-CLASS WOMEN SHOT PUTTERS

The two athletes chosen for this comparison are: Judy Oakes (Britain) – personal best of 19.38 at only 5'4"/78kg – Commonwealth gold medallist. Huang Zhihong (China) – personal best of 21.52 at 5'9"/100kg – Double World gold medallist.

Fig 1 Both athletes start from a low position with the spine at or near the horizontal. Note the relaxed manner of both athletes.

Fig 2 The glide is initiated by a controlled over-balancing in the direction of throw with, at the same time, a straightening of the rear leg and a swing/push of the leading leg.

Fig 3 Huang (H3) leaves the back of the circle from the heel of the rear leg which is the more conventional method. Oakes (O3) leaves the rear of the circle by the toe which only a minority of athletes exhibit. (NB – Former world record holder Randy Matson, 21.78 in 1967, also used this method). Care must be taken if the 'toe' method is used since there is a tendency to lose the low body position during the glide, although here Oakes controls the body position admirably. It is important that the athlete ensures that the shoulder axis is kept closed and, although both athletes achieve this, Oakes has a much better use of the left arm which ensures a 'closed' shoulder position. Both athletes exhibit excellent drive with the rear leg and a smooth vigorous low movement of the leading (left) leg.

Fig 4 Both athletes are in the mid-glide phase showing a low fast use of the rear foot. Note how they both keep the shoulders square to the rear with the shot to the right of the near thigh.

Fig 5 & 6 Huang has moved her rear foot quickly enough to ensure a lay back position, whereas Oakes is more centralised over her rear foot and has adopted a slightly more 'open' position than Huang. Note how wide the base is for Oakes considering the height of the athlete.

Fig 7 & 8 Both athletes are driving the hips forward and attempting to leave the shot back. Oakes appears to be drifting forwards whereas Huang is still over her rear leg. Note how both athletes have delayed the arm strike. Perhaps because of an over-wide base Oakes (O7) has not driven far enough over the front foot at this point.

Fig 9 & 10 Both athletes exhibit tremendous power. Oakes' extension of her left leg when the body weight is not over the foot causes the shot to be released to the rear of the stop board, therefore losing range. Both athletes have attempted to block their left side to ensure that the final arm strike is both effective and **rangey**.

Fig 11 & 12 Both athletes attempt to chase the shot out of the circle with Huang being more effective. Both athletes reverse to ensure that the foot foul does not occur. The sequence analysed does not begin to convey the speed and flowing power of both athletes which can only be achieved after years and countless hours of training.

H1   H2   H3   H4

H5   H6   H7   H8

H9   H10   H11   H12

O1   O2   O3   O4

O5   O6   O7   O8

O9   O10   O11   O12

Brian Oldfield (U.S.A.) – The first athlete to throw over 22 metres

ROTATIONAL SHOT TECHNIQUE

Grip - Most rotational exponents position the shot further back and higher than for linear throwing, but this aspect is very much a matter of personal experimentation.

Entry

AIM - *To enter the turn **on balance** with optimum speed.*

The athlete should adopt a preliminary stance with his feet slightly wider than shoulder width apart, with the putting arm held out at 90 degrees. (R1+2) During the preliminary swing the athlete must take care not to swing too far to his right and must keep the bodyweight 'centred' between the feet. The athlete sits and transfers his weight to his right side (R1), performing a short swing to the right to obtain rhythm and initial speed. The thrower then sits a little lower and transfers his weight over to his left foot, keeping his torso erect and the putting arm high (R2-4). Next comes a positive turn of the whole body to the left, ensuring that he enters 'on balance' (R5), since any small imbalance at the back of the circle will be magnified in the front half of the circle. The entry into the turn should not be rushed, since

we are looking for optimum speed, not maximum speed. The athlete should remember the concept of slow (back of the circle) to fast (front of the circle). During the entry it might be helpful for the athlete to think of himself being like a hinged door, with his left side being the hinge and the right side being the closing door. It is also beneficial to think of a vertical chin-knee-toe position on entry. Remember, whatever the athlete does at the start of the throw will be exaggerated at the end of the throw.

KEY POINTS
- HIGH PUTTING ELBOW
- ERECT TORSO - DEEP SIT
- LEFT SIDE ON BALANCE
- OPTIMUM SPEED

R1

R2

R3

R4

The Turn

AIM - T*o gather both horizontal and angular velocity and to land in an efficient throwing position.*

In fig. R6 several essential points can be observed. The turn at the back of the circle is initiated by turning of the left foot through the ball of the foot assisted by the later action of a wide right leg. The left foot/knee/shoulder which entered the turn in line are now facing the direction of the throw. The right foot has performed a wide semi-circle swing and is about to come through to the centre of the circle (R7). By (R8) Oldfield is leaning into the circle which results in a 'mirror image' position later in the throw (R12), the head remaining in one position, the foot moving through to give lateral range. The left arm should be kept long, which slows the upper body and gives torque later in the throw. The left shoulder must be thought of as 'blocking' (slowing/stopping) on entry which allows the right side of the body to accelerate through.

The throwing elbow is kept high throughout the turn to counter the considerable centrifugal force of the shot - an essential point.

The right leg, having swung round at the back of the circle, makes a circular, stepping action into the middle of the circle, and must be controlled due to the restrictive dimensions of the shot circle. The power of the turn is a combination of the afore-mentioned right leg action and the left leg which pushes/flicks (R9-10) off the back of the circle. The left leg must travel to the front quickly and follow a linear path.

The sequence photographs (R10) and (R11) represent a critical point in the movement, since the longer the left foot is in the air, the less efficient the throw will be, and the all-important torque position (hips ahead of shoulders) will be lost in the power position (R12). The thrower should land on the ball of his right foot (R10) and continue turning on the ball of the foot; do not ground the whole of the foot at this point since this would stop the whole flow of the throw. The left arm is kept long, low and relaxed to assist the torque - long radius of the upper body reducing speed - short radius of the lower body increasing speed.

The base of the rotational thrower will be somewhat less than that of the linear thrower, due to the smallness of the circle when using a turn rather than a glide; *but* a small base is an advantage to the rotational thrower, since it will enable him to use both legs to produce vertical lift.

KEY POINTS

- HIGH ELBOW
- FAST LEFT LEG
- LONG LEFT ARM
- RIGHT FOOT TURNING

R5

R6

Power Position

AIM - *A balanced torqued position.*

Photograph (R12) is a critical position and its effectiveness is judged at the moment the left leg grounds at the front of the circle. To obtain an early grounding of the left foot the athlete must ensure that the right foot turns up on grounding in the centre of the circle.

The athlete must land in a *'torqued'* position (R12) with the right side of the body kept moving by the rotating right foot. Note the torqued position, with the hips leading the shoulders and possessing stored kinetic energy from the entry and turn. The left arm is still long, ensuring that the left shoulder is in a closed position. Oldfield exhibits good leanback which adds range to the throw.

You will notice that Oldfield's foot placement is perfectly aligned (R12), although a slight blocked position is of no real disadvantage since the primary aim of the athlete is to lift, not push, the hips through to the front. It assists the blocking of the left side.

From (R12) to (R14) there has been a horizontal drift, taking the centre of gravity from over the rear leg to between the feet, which will help the athlete to lift off both legs. The athlete must develop this 'drift', possibly by getting himself to 'feel' the power position for a split second before lifting with the legs.

KEY POINTS
- TORQUED POSITION
- FEET IN LINE
- DRIFT

R7

R8

R9

R10

The Throw - (Legs)

AIM - *To give the shot as much velocity as possible.*

The final throwing movement must be very much a leg dominated movement. The delivery is really an unwinding upwards movement after landing in the power position with the shot 'in the pocket' - to right of the right hip (R12). In photograph (R14) Oldfield is seen starting a tremendous lifting movement using *both* legs. The action is very different to that of the linear style, where it is the right leg which is primarily concerned with the pushing through of the hips. Here initially there is only a slight forward push of the hips. The rotation of the whole throwing movement, started at the back of the circle, will ensure that the hips will go forward and the athlete should therefore concentrate on the lifting action of the legs. The athlete should think of the final action as being performed with the hips.

The left arm is now brought in close and fast, thus helping to accelerate the upper body, but it must not be taken too far back. It is essential that the left side is stopped (blocked) so that the right throwing side can accelerate against it. It is much easier to obtain this block if the left foot is 'in line' after the turn. Both feet turn into the throw and the right side goes through into the throw.

KEY POINTS

- TWO LEG LIFT
- LEFT SIDE BLOCK

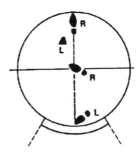

Foot Placements Compared

Fig. 30

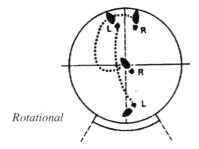

Rotational

Linear

R11

R12

R13

R14

R15

R16

R17

R18

R19

The Throw - (Arm)

AIM - *To give an already fast moving object further speed.*

By photograph (R17) the legs have completed their explosive task, and such is their effectiveness that Oldfield is forced to leave contact with the circle before the shot is released. The arm comes in late and fast, with the elbow high and behind the shot. Note that the blocking action of (R17) has carried through and the arm can strike from a firm, if airborne platform. (R18) is a remarkable photograph illustrating the dynamic power of Oldfield. Although the action of pushing the right hand will create the reaction from the shot of pushing the athlete backwards, thus losing a little range, the only way Oldfield could avoid leaving the circle would be by using less leg power, thereby losing a lot of distance.

Throughout the arm strike Oldfield looks forward and upwards in line with his angle of delivery, and continues this in (R19) during his recovery with a rotational reverse. The athlete should have no problems with fouling at the front of the circle if (a) he has blocked his left side strongly and (b) his leg lift has been vertical.

KEY POINTS
- ARM FAST AND LAST

Seen from the side

Oldfield exhibits a low balanced pre-entry position.

He endeavours to keep the right foot turning and ground the left foot as quickly as possible.

40

The power position – note the lay back and torque.

Oldfield drifts forward to allow his bodyweight to centre between his two feet.

The tremendous leg drive has finished – note the excellent block of the left side.

He chases the shot out of the circle.

LINEAR AND ROTATIONAL TECHNIQUES COMPARED

It is a common misconception that the advantage of using rotational shot is because the path of the shot is longer into the power position and therefore the shot is moving faster at that point. As you can observe from the graphs below, both techniques have similar velocity readings at the time the power position is assumed (3). The long path of the rotational shot putter may well build up stored energy at this point which can be released into the shot during the throw.

LINEAR

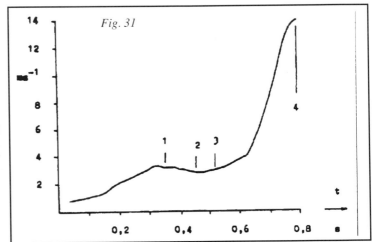

Fig. 31

Ulf Timmermann 21.32m.. Movement of the shot plotted by speed and time: (1) breaking of contact with rear of circle, (2) placement of rear foot, (3) placing front foot, (4) release of shot.

ROTATIONAL

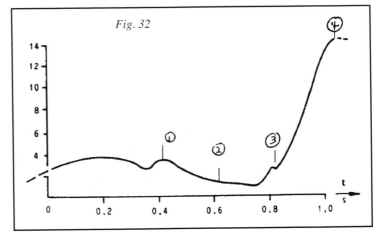

Fig. 32

Movement of shot plotted by speed in a Dave Laut (U.S.A.) 21.56 throw

ROTATIONAL VARIATIONS

Rotational - *linear*

With this method Baryshnikov (RUS) became the first man officially to exceed 22 metres. The thrower rotates to the power position using a 'step' like action (as opposed to the more discus-like rotation of Oldfield), and from the power position (Fig. 33) imitates the linear putting action, driving in the right hip and blocking the left side. It is difficult to see the advantage of this method over linear, since at the power position the shot speed is not greater than with the linear, and indeed a balanced position may be more difficult to achieve.

Aleksandr Baryshnikov (RUS), the first rotational thrower to win Olympic medals.

Fig. 33

ROTATIONAL DRILLS

Modified standing throw

It is of very little use to perform conventional linear standing puts, since the action of the rotational exponent is radically different. The athlete adopts the position he would arrive in, in the power position (Dr.1.), both legs bent, shot over or just inside the rear leg. From this position the athlete must lift with both legs, with much less right hip drive than the linear thrower. He must also attempt to block the left side. The two essential elements are LIFT and BLOCK. The thrower attempts to throw the shot high, rather than the more horizontal drive of the linear style.

Half-turn Drill

The starting position is with the right foot in the centre of the circle and the left foot about 80 cms to the rear. The thrower is wound up (Dr.2). He then pushes off the left leg vigorously to initiate a fast right foot pivot, so that the left foot is out of contact with the ground for as short a time as possible. Dr. 3 demonstrates the mid position. When the left foot grounds at the front of the circle, the athlete then performs the lifting/blocking movement.

Dr. 1

Dr. 2

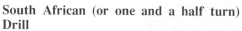
Dr. 4

South African (or one and a half turn) Drill

The thrower starts with his left foot at the back of the circle as for a normal turn, but 180 degrees round. The right foot is outside the circle, as far from the left foot as is comfortable. The athlete is in a wound-up position (Dr. 4). He initiates the movement by moving his bodyweight over the left leg and then driving off it. The right leg is relaxed and follows an arc to the centre of the circle. The athlete arrives in the power position and finishes the throw.

Dr. 3

Teaching the Novice – Linear Shot Put

Stage One

It is essential that from the very outset the correct grip is taught for, however efficient the rest of the throw is, if the grip is incorrect the distance thrown will be disappointing. With an incorrect grip it is likely that the athlete will hurt himself/herself and thereby lose confidence.

The shot should be placed at the base of the first three fingers (Fig.34a) with the little finger and thumb giving support at the sides of the shot. The shot should then be placed under the chin with the elbow held high (Fig.34b). A simple way for the novice to acquire the correct grip is to place the shot on the floor, then grip the shot from above lifting the implement to the chin/neck.

Fig. 34a

Stage Two

Having established the correct grip, the novice should be quickly put into a very simple throwing position to test his grip and thereby given confidence. Pupils should be placed along a line with feet shoulder width apart, facing the direction of the throw.

Fig. 34b

a   b   c   d

Fig. 35
Standing frontal put,
not using legs.

Fig. 36
Standing frontal put,
using legs.

Fig. 37

elbow up *(thumb down)* behind the shot and following the shot right out with a fast arm action (Fig39). The left shoulder must not be allowed to drop during any part of this movement and the thrower should think of keeping the left side braced (Fig. 39) *(watch it go)*.

THINK

    – CHIN-KNEE-TOE

    – MAKE A BOW*

    – WATCH IT GO

*The effect of pushing the hips forward ahead of the shoulders will cause a 'bow-like' shape to the body prior to release.

Stage Three

The thrower should be given the formal standing put stance (Fig 37a) and should be encouraged to think of 'chin-knee-toe' being in line vertically with the feet/hips facing the side and the shoulder "cocked" to the rear – how far to the rear depends upon the strength of the athlete. The width of the stance should vary according to the height of the youngster (60-90 cms), but care should be taken so that the toes of the left foot are in line with the heel of the right foot (Fig 38). From this standing put position *(chin-knee-toe)* the thrower should commence the movement by the right leg pushing the hips to the front. During this action the emphasis should be on a fast right hip *(making the bow)*, keeping the

Stage Four

Place the standing put skill directly into a competition. Once it has been mastered, encourage the thrower to try for greater distance by adopting any form of "shift" between two lines about 7ft. (2.135 metres) apart. At this stage it would be wrong to:

(i) use an orthodox circle with a stopboard, since this would inhibit freedom of movement and hamper the final putting movement.

(ii) teach the advanced glide technique, since this takes very many hours of practice and when first introduced may lead to a temporary reduction in distance. Keener pupils should be encouraged to attend special school/club sessions to learn a

47

more orthodox style which will eventually lead to a modified O'Brien shift, and to join the local club for extra help.

The initial movement should be one of free choice, but it should be emphasised that the thrower must arrive ready for the final action in the "chin-knee-toes" position, with the elbow high behind the shot. The movement between the lines can be a simple side shuffle, side step, step back, etc. (Figs 40-42). The emphasis is on distance through increased speed of movement.

Fig. 38

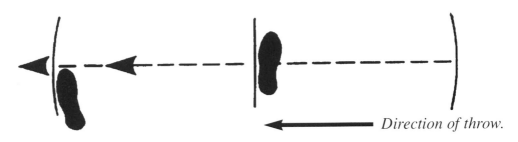

Direction of throw.

Fig. 39

a   b   c   d   e   f   g   h

Fig.40 – Walk technique – backwards action

Fig.41 – Walk technique – two stride action

Fig.42 – Glide technique – sideways action

Training for Shot

The following statistics are taken from recent Olympic Games and are the average measurements of the finalists:

	MEN			WOMEN		
	Age (y)	Weight (kg)	Height (m)	Age (y)	Weight (kg)	Height (m)
1980	28.25	130.5	1.95	26.25	89	1.755
1984*	24.75	110.5	1.925	26.5	86.5	1.77
1988	27.5	125	1.92	27.5	92	1.80
1992	28.25	117.5	1.915	25.5	94	1.795
Average	27.25	120.75	1.9275	25.75	90.5	1.78

Boycotted Olympics: since the former Eastern Bloc were absent the figures quoted are perhaps not indicative of world levels that year.

The above statistics indicate that shot athletes are physically abnormal, but these figures do not indicate the power, the skill, the suppleness of world class throwers. Great strength and size are not enough, and the coach and athlete must strive to achieve excellence in all facets of fitness. The following German tables give an indication of the levels of power needed to throw specific distances:

GERMAN SPECIFIC TESTS FOR SELECTION – DISTANCES THROWN
Abstracted from the book Throwing and Putting - H. Gundlach (1991)

Shot – Men

7.25kg	(m)	17.00 (5.0kg)	17.00 (6.25kg)	17.50	19.50	20.80	23.00
Shot 8kg	(m)	–	–	–	17.50	18.80	20.90
Shot 7.25kg overhead	(m)	15.00	16.25	18.25	20.00	21.00	22.70
30m Flying	(s)	3.3	3.2	3.15	3.10	3.20	3.30
Three Jumps	(m)	8.90	9.40	9.80	10.20	10.20	10.00
Back Squat	(kg)	125	135	155	180	200	250
Bench Press	(kg)	105	120	145	170	185	250
Push Press	(kg)	80	100	127.5	165	190	240
Snatch	(kg)	75	85	97.5	110	122.5	145

Shot – Women

4kg	(m)	13.75	15.50	17.50	18.50	20.50	22.50
Shot 5kg	(m)	–	–	–	16.00	18.50	20.30
Shot 4kg overhead	(m)	15.00	16.00	17.50	18.50	20.50	22.50
30m Flying	(s)	3.7	3.6	3.5	3.4	3.45	3.50
Three Jumps	(m)	7.70	8.20	8.70	8.20	9.40	9.20
Back Squat	(kg)	85	100	115	130	150	180
Bench Press	(kg)	70	82.5	95	105	125	160
Push Press	(kg)	60	70	85	100	125	145
Snatch	(kg)	55	60	67.5	75	90	110

THE FIVE S's

Skill

The old adage *'Technique first – sweat second'* holds good for all throwing events. Specific technique practices should always be performed when the athlete is fresh, and under no circumstances must the athlete be allowed to throw poorly due to fatigue. Technique work must, then, occur early in the session. It is good practice to allow the athlete to perform his/her throws in sets, allowing a few minutes rest after say 15 puts and a further few minutes rest after a further 10 puts. In this way a long session can be composed of quality throws. It is not the quantity of throws that is important, but the number of well executed throws which counts.

Major technique changes should always be made during the early winter period, since major changes during the season are usually a recipe for disaster. At the end of the season the athlete should decide on what technical faults he has, and what corrections are necessary. By the time the next season has commenced, the changes should be well established, and only minor refinements prove necessary.

It is important, as far as is practical, to ensure that conditions for throwing are good.

Progress will be much faster if the athlete can throw indoors during the cold, dark winter months. If this is not possible, throw outside when weather permits, but use indoor space for drills when unable to go outside.

The shot put is one dynamic movement and although the technique can be broken down into part techniques, these must always be brought back into the whole. The closer the season comes, the more the whole technique must be the prime consideration, eg.:

Winter throws session
   10 standing fixed feet throws
   10 glide-stop throws
   10 full throws

Summer throws session
   5 standing fixed feet throws
   5 glide-stop throws
   20 full throws

Although the athlete's technique may have several faults, it is a mistake to try and correct them all at once. An attempt must be made to assess the main fault and correct that. No matter how talented the athlete, you can only work on one correction at a time. Many apparent faults are merely symptoms of the cause; you must find the cause, the fault that is the root of negative performances.

Stamina

Novice throwers often undervalue the need to be physically fit to throw the shot elite distances,simply because the execution of the event itself, over a few seconds, requires little in the way of fitness. But it is essential that youngsters quickly acquire strength endurance for two vital areas of training.

(a) **Throwing** – technical improvement can only be achieved when the throwing is of high quality. The more high quality throws the athlete can make in a session the greater the gain will be in technique. Remember, it's not *'practice that makes perfect'* but *'perfect practice makes perfect'*. An unfit athlete will never achieve his technical potential because he will never be able to produce enough quality training throws in his career.

(b) **Strength Training** – the old adage of *'only the last rep counts'* holds true in strength training. If the athlete is performing eight repetitions maximum, then it is the eighth repetition which is the one that will bring about the strength gain. The previous seven repetitions are merely means to an end. An unfit person will quickly fatigue and never enter the region of strength gain, especially in the cardio-vascular lifts such as clean and snatch. There is no easy way to build strength. Long hours are required in the strength room and the fitter the athlete, the more sets and repetitions can be performed.

The initial phase of the training year (Sept/Oct) should be devoted to building an endurance base and should consist of long runs, circuit training and high repetition weights. Never be tempted to cut this phase short since strength gains will be quicker and greater if made on a foundation of fitness. During the rest of the training year care must be taken to ensure that fitness levels are maintained. Fitness work reduces the fat content of the body which is desirable since:

YOU CARRY FAT
MUSCLE CARRIES YOU

Speed

Without doubt the facet which enables athletes to throw world class distances is not size or strength or even technique but SPEED. It is important that explosive power is enhanced by training. General speed and elastic strength can be developed by such activities as sprinting, jumping and explosive use of weight training. For specific shot putting speed the use of underweight shots is essential. The senior thrower who uses a 6.25kg or 6.75kg shot in training will gain the experience of throwing distances that he aspires to. It would be beneficial to use underweight implements throughout the whole year. In winter the session may comprise say 20 full weight throws followed by 10 lighter weight throws, which also gives the added bonus of a change in the session just when the thrower is feeling bored or a little tired. The use of under-weight implements is also useful at times when the coach believes a change would be beneficial. In mid-season, for example, when the athlete is a little stale, he would benefit from two weeks with a lighter shot.

SUPPLENESS

For an athlete to be able to apply force over as great a range as possible, he must improve his technique and also ensure that his mobility is such that he can assume rangey positions. Shot putters are heavy, strong athletes, but if this bulk is achieved at the expense of mobility, then the thrower will not be a better shot putter.

A supple athlete is also less likely to injure himself in his training, hitting extreme ranges in activities such as sprinting, bounding, weight-lifting etc.

It is necessary to perform general mobility exercises every day, if possible as part of the athlete's daily cycle. A convenient way of achieving this is for the athlete to include mobility in his warm-up for training so that it is performed regularly. In addition to this, the athlete should put aside a period of time when he performs specific sessions for mobility. The athlete may have concentrated sessions in early winter to increase his range and thereafter try to maintain this new found mobility.

As with most aspects of fitness, mobility is specific and the ability to touch your toes may not help you to assume a powerful, rangey throwing position. Therefore the athlete should look at the shot action and try to design simulated shot mobility exercises.

The exercises illustrated are examples of mobility exercises related to the shot action. See also the B.A.F. book *Mobility Training*.

MOBILITY EXERCISES

TORSO

SHOULDERS

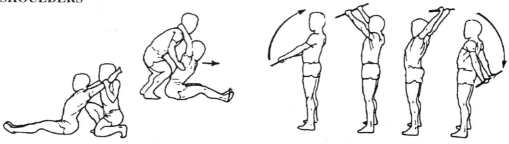

Strength

To put the shot a long way an athlete must be strong. This apparently simple statement does not reveal the complexity of strength training,i.e. what kind of strength? with what? when? how much?

Below I have listed strength levels of a former two-time AAA Junior Champion who went on to gain a medal in the World Powerlifting Championships.

	1974	1977
Bodyweight	240	285
Age	22	26
Bench Press	180kg	220kg
Back Squat	240kg	330kg
Dead Lift	240kg	315kg
Shot Distance (7.26kg)	17.90	16.54

Although less time was spent on throwing. it is obvious that this athlete did not benefit from drastically increasing his ability to lift heavy weights (gross strength). The type of strength acquired was not immediately of use since other strength facets (explosive/elastic strength) had not been developed in parallel. The coach must ensure that the strength schedule designed should reflect the nature of the event which is a combination of gross strength (heavy lifting) and the quick (elastic) strength needed to accelerate the 7.25kg shot to 14 metres per second within the confines of a seven foot circle in less than a second. That kind of strength is a very special kind of strength!

Initially the young athlete should go through a long period of conditioning before commencing weight-lifting. This would include circuit training, bodyweight exercises and multi-gym exercises which may well, depending upon his maturity, take him into his mid to late teens. To commence lifting heavy barbells at too young an age, without prior strength conditioning, may lead to injuries, especially when over-loading the spine and knee areas before final skeletal ossification.

It is the author's opinion that the lifting of barbells and dumbbells is the tried and tested and almost certainly the best method of gaining gross strength for throwing. There is not a world class shot putter who has not spent a considerable period of time lifting weights!

The bulk of the hours spent lifting will be spent pulling, squatting and pressing since these movements involve the major muscle groups used in shot putting:

PULLING
Power Clean (PC 1-4) and/or Power Snatch (P. S. 1-6)

PUSHING
Bench Press (BP 1-4) Press, etc

SQUATTING
Back Squat (BS 1-3) Front Squat, Jump Squat etc.

**BENCH
PRESS**

BP1

BP2

BP3

BP4

THE SQUAT

BS1

BS2

BS3

THE POWER CLEAN

PC1   PC2

PC3   PC4

THE POWER SNATCH

PS1

PS2

PS3

PS4

PS5

PS6

In addition the athlete must not neglect the torso trunk area and exercises such as sit-ups, side bends and hyper-extensions must always feature in the weekly schedule.

The above basic exercises will form the bulk of the strength programme but there is a need in addition for the coach to look for specialist exercises that will isolate the muscles actually involved in the throwing movement.

The incline press (opposite) is an example of highly specific movement. Since the shot will be released at between 35°-42° the regular bench press would develop strength at 0°. Raising the bench to say 40° would make the movement relate to the release angle, thus developing the deltoids, pectorals, triceps etc in the exact relationship desired. Using dumbbells instead of barbells would be even more specific since the range of movement would be increased.

Below are several exercises that develop those muscle groups concerned in shot putting.

IP1

IP2

When performing exercises a critical decision to make is how many repetitions of each exercise must be performed. Once the athlete has become familiar with weights he will formulate a schedule that will show changes as the training year progresses. As a rule of thumb, at the start of the winter the repetitions will be high (8-10) and progressively, in a series of steps, reduce as the season approaches. An example of how the choice of the system of repetitions may change can be seen as follows:

October   *– Sets of 8-12*
November/December   *– Sets of 6-8*
January/March   *– Sets of 4-5*
April   *– Sets of 1-3*
May   *– Sets of explosive 5 reps.*

Elastic Strength Exercises
Gains in gross strength are relatively easily attained, but the activity of shot putting does not always correlate highly with increases in gross strength. It is the amount of elastic (explosive) strength present that dictates the distance thrown.

Elastic Strength can be increased via:
(a) Weight-training – by executing each lift in a dynamic fashion, eg. 5 reps in 6 seconds. Lifts suitable for this regime are Jump Squats, Bench Press, Clean from Hang, Snatch from Hang, Push Press, etc.
(b) Jumping – eg. standing long jump, bounding, depth jumping. Care must be taken since throwers may be susceptible to injury when performing high repetition bounding, due to heavy bodyweight.
(c) Throwing heavy weights – too heavy a weight may cause a deterioration in both technique and timing. For full technique work it is better to use not more than 15% more than the competitive weight. If heavier weights are to be used, the athlete should be restricted to using simple standing throws only and possibly from a fixed feet position.

In the period immediately prior to competition (final 4-6 weeks) this linking of gross and elastic strength is vital and a session such as follows may lead to improvement:
1.   Bench Press -
     4 sets of 5 reps (fast), super-setted with medicine ball push - 6 reps.
2.   Bench Squat -
     4 sets of 6 reps (fast), super-setted with hurdle bounding - 6 reps.
3   Clean -
     4 sets of 4 reps (fast), super-setted with overhead medicine ball throw.

N.B. Super-set: two exercises performed one after another without rest, to form one set.

In the competitive season the volume of strength training will reduce to allow for quality work in other areas. Strength levels must be kept high and 2-3 strength units per week should still be included, but the athlete must not leave the session absolutely drained of energy. The aim is to maintain, not gain. Experience indicates that even the day before a competition a light weights sessions using 60% of normal poundage may give both muscle tone and confidence to the athlete.

Torso Conditioning
It is a cause for concern that far too many athletes finish their athletic careers with chronic back injuries. Throwing is as much a rotational movement as it is a vertical or horizontal movement, but athletes perform great volumes of vertical lifting with little or no rotational movements. This will eventually leave the athlete susceptible to injury when performing rotational movements. Medicine ball work is a pleasant activity that should form an integral part of every thrower's routine. Exercises should be performed in sets of 8-12 repetitions for 20-30 minutes with emphasis given in the early winter period.

Medicine Ball Torso Exercises

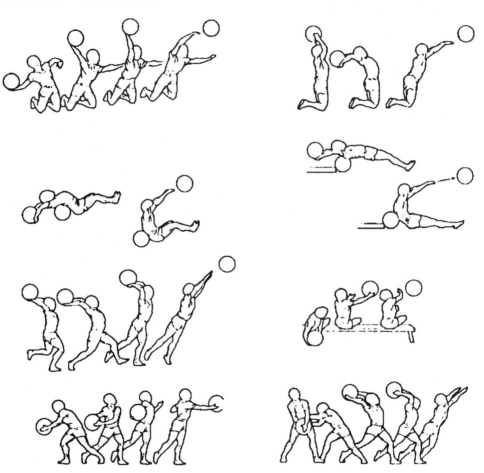

Maintaining the Balance

Having discussed the elements that go to make up the shot putter's schedule, the coach/athlete has next to decide on putting them together into a schedule. The problem is how much and when, for the schedule must be continually changing to reflect the time of year and the status of the athlete. The schedule is not a once-a-year document since it frequently changes with the seasons of the year; the more advanced the athlete, the more'fine tuning' is required. The novice needs a more basic programme that will be more static. Before giving examples of schedules it is important to stress that *all* athletes, whether beginner or international, will need to perform a warm-up routine that will ensure that the body is ready to perform at a high level *and* be less susceptible to injury. The following sequence of activities should be indoctrinated into the athlete as early in his career as possible.

1. Jog – to raise the body temperature. The distance will vary from 400m to 1200m.
2. Strides – two or three repetitions of 40-60 metres with a walk back recovery.
3. General stretching exercises.
4. Specific stretching exercises for shot.
5. A few easy, relaxed throws.

This regime will put the athlete into condition to commence either his training schedule or a competition. Too few athletes remember that it is also important to warm down, (1) to remove the accumulated waste products derived from intensive training, and (2) to reflect on lessons learned from the session or competition. The warm-down takes less time than the warm-up and stages 1-4 can be reversed with less exercises and repetitions performed.

Sample Schedules

A novice fourteen year old shot putter may well have the following simple general schedule to follow:

	Winter (October-April)	Summer (May-August)
Sun	(i) Throwing – 20 throws (10 standing – 10 full)	(i) Technique work – 30 throws (6 standing – 12 full) – 5 mins rest, followed by 12 full throws
	(ii) Second event work, eg 5 runs over 4 flights of hurdles	(ii) Discus – 12 throws (iii) Sprinting – 30m x 5
Mon	Rest	Rest
Tues	(i) 20 mins stretching at club-based session	(i) Throwing – 20 throws (6 standing – 14 full)
	(ii) Circuit training – general nature	(ii) Sprinting – 60m x 4
Wed	Rest	Rest
Thurs	(i) Basic technique work – drills – indoors	(i) Throwing – 20 throws (6 standing – 14 full)
	(ii) Circuit training – general	(ii) Long jumping (6 stride approach x 8)
Fri	—	—
Sat	School match	Club/School competion

The coach must always ascertain the amount of school-based physical education performed by the athlete. A good games player could take part in 5-6 hours of strenuous activity at school and the coach must adjust the schedule accordingly. The average fourteen year old would almost certainly have his endurance background taken up by his school PE programme.

For the *novice* athlete the schedule should be:

(i)   simple
(ii) not too event specific (an all-round athlete is the aim)
(iii) not too demanding on time and energy

At this stage the sport should be fun and not too disciplined, hopefully motivating the athlete to take the sport seriously.

Intermediate

As the youngster progresses, he will decide upon which event he will specialise in. This must not occur at too early a stage, since working at and experiencing a whole range of events will give a solid wide base of conditioning and techniques, onto which a successful shot put career can be built. At the point of specialisation it is likely that team sports and compulsory physical education will have been dropped and therefore the coach must assume responsibility for the whole programme. By the age of 18 the novice schedule may have been developed as shown in Table A.

TABLE A

SAMPLE SCHEDULE FOR 18 YEAR OLD OF SEVERAL YEARS' EXPERIENCE

	Strength	Specific Strength	Elastic Strength	Endurance	Technique	Rest days
Sept/Oct (6 weeks)	general exercises 3-4 sets of 8-12 reps (x 3/wk)	medicine ball work – high reps working on rotational strength (x 1/wk)	—	4000m steady run or 30 mins cycling or conditioning body-weight circuits (x 3/week)	(x 1 week)	2
Nov/Dec	basic lifts – 4 sets of 6 rising to 8, then adding weight (x 3/wk)	as above (x 1/wk)	bounding – 8 sets of 3 bunnies (x 1/wk). 60m fast strides (5 reps) (x 2/wk)	3000m steady run (x 1/wk)	indoor throwing (x 1 wk) outdoor (x 1/wk)	2
Jan/Mar	basic lifts – 4 sets of 4, rising to 6, then adding weight (x 3/wk)	medicine ball (x 1/week) heavy shot (8.0kg) from stand x 15 (x 1/wk)	bounding – bunnies plus 2 x 5 reps standing long jump (x 1/week) 40m sprint x 5 reps (x 1/wk)	2000m at good pace (x 1/wk)	indoor throwing (x 1/wk) outdoor (x 2/wk)	2
April/May	as for Jan/Mar – reduced volume (x 3/wk)	as Jan/March	bounding – 6 x 2 bunnies, plus 2 sets of 5 standing long jump (x 2/wk) 40m x 5 reps (x 2/wk)	—	outdoor (x 2/wk)	1
Jun/Aug	moderate poundage – weights handled explosively (x 1/2wk)	—	bounding as for April/ May (x 2/wk) sprints (x 1/wk)	—	outdoor (x 5/wk)	1

NB – multiple units

63

TABLE B

THE ADVANCED THROWER – AN OUTLINE SCHEDULE

Phases	1¹ (Nov-Dec)	2¹ (Jan)	3¹ (Feb-mid-Mar)	1² (Mid Mar-April)	2² (May)
PERIODS	PREPARATION	PREPARATION	COMP	PREPARATION	PREPARATION
Strength	Many exercises – basically 3 sets of 10 reps, moving to 4 sets of 8 reps by end of phase (x 3/wk)	Mixture of 75%-85% work, moving to 85%-95% work; major muscle group work (x 3-5/wk)	Lower volume – explosive work, eg 5 reps in 6 secs (x 3/wk)	75%-85% of work (x 3/wk)	85%-95% work – lower volume near end of phase (x 3-4/wk)
Explosive/ Elastic Strength	Medicine ball work – high reps, many exercises (2 x /wk)	Bounding – 6-8 foot contacts (x 2/wk). Medicine ball work – 10 reps, heavy ball (x 1/wk)	Quality bounding, 2/3 foot contacts (x 2/wk) (early part)	Bounding – 6 foot contacts x 1/wk. Medicine ball work – 8 reps (x 1/wk)	Bounding – 3 foot contacts (x 2/wk)
Specific Strength		Heavy shot work, 8-9kg standing puts (x 2/wk)		Heavy shot work as for phase 2	—
Technique	Major skill changes, light shot (eg 6.25kg men) (2 x /wk)	shots of variable weights + / – 10% of comp weight (x 3/wk)	comp. work, standard and light (6.75) shots (x 4/wk)	comp work – variable weights + / –10% (x 4/wk)	comp work – standard and light (6.75) shots (x 5/wk)
Runs	4000m jog (x 1/wk) 6 x 100m strides (x 2/wk)	6 x 100m (x 1/wk) 6 x 30m (indoors) (x 1/wk)	4 x 30m – indoor – timed (x 1/wk)	4 x 150m easy strides (x 1/wk)	6 x 30m x (1/wk) 4 x 60m x (1/wk)
Mobility	Specific session (x 2/wk) aiming to improve weak spots + normal everyday session	Every day regime, eg incorporated in warm-up			

Phases	3² (June)	4 (July)	5 (Aug-Sept)	6 (Oct)
PERIODS		COMPETITION		TRANSITION
Strength	explosive work – 5 reps/6 secs sandwiched (super-setted) with stretch reflex work (x 3/wk)	lower volume explosive work (1 x3/wk)	as 3b	(at the end of the competitive season) Three weeks of active rest, eg swimming, squash, jogging, etc
Explosive/ Elastic Strength	low volume high quality 1-2 foot contact (x 2/wk)	Bounding – 3-4 foot contacts (x 1/wk)	as 3b	
Specific Strength	—	—	—	
Technique	comp weight shot work (x 5/wk)	6.75kg shots work – quality (x 3/wk)	repeat 3²	
Runs	4 x 30m timed (x 1/wk)	4 x 60m fast strides (x 2/wk)	repeat 3²	
Mobility	Everyday regime eg incorporated in warm-up			

65

Advanced

It is now important that the coach looks at the year in detail and phases the programme. Division of the athletic year into separate training periods is called PERIODISATION.

Single Periodised Year

months	Nov	Dec	Jan	Feb	Mar	Apr	May	Jun	Jul	Aug	Sep	Oct
phases	1				2		3		4		5	6
periods	preparation						competition					trans-ition

Double Periodised Year

months	Nov	Dec	Jan	Feb	Mar	Apr	May	Jun	Jul	Aug	Sep	Oct
phases	1_1		2_1	3_1	1_2		2_2	3_2	4		5	6
periods	preparation			compet-ition	preparation			competition				trans-ition

The phasing-periodising of the year against the months indicated is a suggestion for illustration. Commencement of the 'year' will vary according to individual circumstances and requirements.

The aim of periodisation is to ensure that a firm base or foundation is established before more specific work is attempted. The foundation or preparation phases consist of high volume/low intensity general work, which gradually changes to the competitive phase when the volume is low and the intensity high. It is important not to have sudden changes, but to ensure that each phase blends into the next.

To plan the training year, the coach should follow several simple planning steps which are:

(1) Decide which competitions are important, since this will naturally form the competitive phase.

(2) Working back through the year, decide how to divide the year into preparation, competition and transition phases.

(3) Decide the needs of the particular athlete and then sub-divide each phase with the aspects of fitness required. All will be included, but with varying importance depending upon the phase, eg in the preparation phase, strength is very important and takes a lot of the time, whereas in the competition phase it becomes far less important.

(4) Decide which methods are to be used to develop the physical qualities in each phase.

(5) The athlete's personal commitment and time available will have to be assessed.

(6) Formulate the training schedule.

Table B on pages 64/65 outlines an example of a periodised year of a thrower of Great Britain International standard.

Major Games Competitor

It is now worth looking at the advanced schedule of a major Games winner starting with the table showing how the intensity of training varies and is planned for:

Year Plan

	10 Weeks	10 Weeks	10 Weeks	Competition
Period	Oct 4 – Dec 9	Dec 10 – Mar 6	Mar 7 – May 9	May 10
Intensity	65%	100%	85%	50%

10 Week Plan

Week	1	2	3	4	5	6	7	8	9	10
Intensity	100%	85%	50%	100%	85%	50%	100%	85%	50%	Rest

Weekly Plan

Day	Mon	Tue	Wed	Thur	Fri	Sat	Sun
Intensity	100%	85%	50%	Rest	100%	85%	50%

Each weekly phase is composed of a weekly cycle which is a repetition of the preceding one. At the end of the phase the athlete is free to do what he feels or wants to do for one week without any interference from the coach or anybody else. If he does not want to do anything, he is free to do so.

The following examples are of the work completed on a three day cycle followed by a day of rest and then repeated.

October 4th - December 9th

Monday (5 hours)	Sprints
	Technique – 140 repetitions (drills plus throws)
	Strength work-out
Tuesday (2 hours)	Extensive warm-up
	Technique - 30 throws
	Strength exercises
	Cross-country run (4000 metres)
Wednesday (1½ hours)	Bounding (40 minutes)
	Games
	Sauna
	Swimming

December 10th - March 6th

Monday (5 hours)	Sprints
	Technique - 60 throws
	Strength (13 exercises)
Tuesday (4 hours)	Extensive warm-up
	Technique - 50 throws

	Strength pyramids (4x6 @ 65 %; 3x3 @ 85 %; 3x1 @ 95 %; 2x6 @ 65 %)
	Four exercises
Wednesday (2 hours)	Games
	Sauna
	Swimming

March 7th - May 9th

Monday (5 hours)	Sprints
	Throwing - 50 throws
	Strength - low repetitions maximum intensity
Tuesday (4 hours)	Extensive warm-up
	Technique – 60 throws (4kg + 6.25kg shots)
	Strength 85% intensity
	Cross country – 3000 metres
Wednesday	General games
	Sauna
	Swimming

The following seven-day cycle was followed tor the period **May 10 - August 30th**

Sunday (4 hours)	Warm-up
	Technique - 40 puts - 6.25kg
	Down hill sprints 5x60 metres
	Strength - power weights
Tuesday (2 hours)	Technique - 50 puts - 6.25kg
	Fast strides 6x90 metres
	Easy run - 2000 metres
Wednesday (1 hour)	General games
	Swim
	Sauna
Thursday (3 hours)	Warm-up
	Technique – 20 throws 7.25kg
	Strength – maximum singles
Friday	Rest
Saturday ($1\frac{1}{2}$ hours)	Easy throws - 20 repetitions
	High load weight training
Sunday	compete – 21.18 metres

Evaluating Your Thrower

The only true measurement is the event itself, but other measurements of physical performance can provide the athlete with motivation and the coach with information relating to the state of fitness of his athlete at any time of the year. The following statistics for Judy Oakes (Commonwealth gold medallist) show how many simple ways there are to evaluate one's progress:

Height	5' 4"	Weight	170 lbs
30m sprint	4.01	Standing Long Jump	2.57
Standing Triple Jump	7.49	Three Bounds	7.76
Five Bounds	12.78	Barbell Clean	117½ kg
Snatch	87½ kg	Clean & Jerk	110 kg
Bench Press (touch)	120 kg	Bench Press (pause at chest)	115 kg
Narrow Grip Bench	117 kg	Incline Bench Press	100 kg
Back Squat	207½ kg	Front Squat	147½ kg
Dead-lift	215 kg		

Training shot marks:

3.25kg 20.43	4 kg 18.47	5 kg	15.57
6.25kg 13.36	7.26 kg 12.43	Overhead shot	18.32

No test is a substitute for the event itself, and often the correlation is a poor one as a Polish study indicates (exercises ranked on a scale of 1 to 100 testing the exercise relationship to shot putting).

Five alternate bounds	90	Back squats	75
Bench press	72	Power clean	68
Vertical jump	67	Clean and jerk	58
Overhead throw	58		

The most popular battery of tests currently used in the UK is the "Test Quadrathlon". Detailed scoring tables are given on page 71 with the following target scores being the incentive.

	Elite	International	Regional	Club
Men	325 +	290	265	240
Women	265 +	240	225	200

BRITISH BEST QUADRATHLON SCORES (SHOT)

	BEST PERFORMANCE	3 JUMPS	SLJ	30M	OHS	PTS
Men						
Mike Winch	20.43	10.31	3.12	3.56	18.57	338
Matt Simson	19.09 (Jnr)	9.42	3.03	3.59	19.06	322
Women						
Judy Oakes	19.36	7.22	2.55	4.01	17.88	256
Maggie Lynes	16.55 (Jnr)	7.67	2.55	3.94	16.08	253

TEST QUADRATHLON

How it Works

Standing Long Jump
Place feet over the edge of the sandpit. The athlete crouches, leans forward, swings his arms backwards, then jumps horizontally as far as possible, jumping from both feet into a sandpit (which should be level with take-off). Measure (metric) to the nearest point of contact.
N.B. The start of the jump must be from a static position.

Three Jumps
Start with the feet comfortably apart with toes just behind the take-off mark. The athlete takes three *continuous* two-footed bounds into the sandpit (level with take-off).
N.B. Spikes allowed. Static start – feet must be parallel on each jump phase.

30 Metre Sprint
On the command the athlete moves to the set position. On the start signal he sprints from a *stationary* set position as fast as possible to the finish line. The time-keeper stands at the finish and times the run from the moment that the runner's foot contacts the ground on the first running stride to the moment when the runner's torso crosses the line. Spikes allowed. Hand times.

Overhead Shot Throw
The athlete stands on the shot stopboard, facing away from the landing area, with his feet a comfortable distance apart. The shot is held cupped in both hands. He crouches, lowering the shot between his legs, then drives upwards to cast the shot back over his head. There is no penalty for following through, but the thrower must land feet first and remain upright. Measurements (to the nearest cm) are taken from the inside of the stopboard. Implements are as per BAF age group. Please watch the safety aspect.

Practical uses
Both athlete and coach can use the Quadrathlon to gauge whether he/she is becoming more powerful, and the benefits are threefold:
(1) If the athlete's score increases, then his power has increased.
(2) Weaknesses can be identified if the athlete 'underscores' and these areas can be worked on.
(3) Motivation help during the long winter months.

TEST QUADRATHLON TABLES (1992)

Points	3 Jumps	SLJ	30m	OH Shot	Points	3 Jumps	SLJ	30m	OH Shot
1	3.00	1.00	5.80	4.00	51	7.04	2.36	4.38	12.58
2	3.08	1.02	5.77	4.17	52	7.12	2.39	4.35	12.75
3	3.16	1.05	5.74	4.34	53	7.20	2.41	4.33	12.92
4	3.24	1.08	5.71	4.51	54	7.28	2.44	4.30	13.10
5	3.32	1.10	5.68	4.68	55	7.36	2.47	4.27	13.27
6	3.40	1.13	5.66	4.85	56	7.44	2.50	4.24	13.44
7	3.48	1.16	5.63	5.03	57	7.52	2.52	4.21	13.61
8	3.56	1.19	5.60	5.20	58	7.60	2.55	4.18	13.78
9	3.64	1.21	5.57	5.37	59	7.68	2.58	4.16	13.95
10	3.72	1.24	5.54	5.54	60	7.76	2.60	4.13	14.13
11	3.80	1.27	5.51	5.71	61	7.84	2.63	4.10	14.30
12	3.88	1.30	5.49	5.88	62	7.92	2.66	4.07	14.47
13	3.96	1.32	5.46	6.06	63	8.01	2.69	4.04	14.64
14	4.05	1.35	5.43	6.23	64	8.09	2.71	4.02	14.81
15	4.13	1.38	5.40	6.40	65	8.17	2.74	3.99	14.98
16	4.21	1.40	5.37	6.57	66	8.25	2.77	3.96	15.16
17	4.29	1.43	5.34	6.74	67	8.33	2.80	3.93	15.33
18	4.37	1.46	5.32	6.91	68	8.41	2.82	3.90	15.50
19	4.45	1.49	5.29	7.09	69	8.49	2.85	3.87	15.67
20	4.53	1.51	5.26	7.26	70	8.57	2.88	3.85	15.84
21	4.61	1.54	5.23	7.43	71	8.65	2.90	3.82	16.02
22	4.69	1.57	5.20	7.60	72	8.73	2.93	3.79	16.19
23	4.77	1.60	5.17	7.77	73	8.81	2.96	3.76	16.36
24	4.85	1.62	5.15	7.94	74	8.89	2.99	3.73	16.53
25	4.93	1.65	5.12	8.12	75	8.97	3.01	3.70	16.70
26	5.02	1.68	5.09	8.29	76	9.06	3.04	3.68	16.87
27	5.10	1.70	5.06	8.46	77	9.14	3.07	3.65	17.05
28	5.18	1.73	5.03	8.63	78	9.22	3.10	3.62	17.22
29	5.26	1.76	5.01	8.80	79	9.30	3.12	3.59	17.39
30	5.34	1.79	4.98	8.97	80	9.38	3.15	3.56	17.56
31	5.42	1.81	4.95	9.15	81	9.46	3.18	3.53	17.73
32	5.50	1.84	4.92	9.32	82	9.54	3.20	3.51	17.90
33	5.58	1.87	4.89	9.49	83	9.62	3.23	3.48	18.03
34	5.66	1.90	4.86	9.66	84	9.70	3.26	3.45	18.23
35	5.74	1.92	4.84	9.83	85	9.78	3.29	3.42	18.42
36	5.82	1.95	4.81	10.01	86	9.86	3.31	3.39	18.59
37	5.90	1.98	4.78	10.18	87	9.94	3.34	3.36	18.76
38	5.98	2.00	4.75	10.35	88	10.03	3.37	3.34	18.93
39	6.07	2.03	4.72	10.52	89	10.11	3.40	3.31	19.11
40	6.15	2.06	4.69	10.69	90	10.19	3.42	3.28	19.28
41	6.23	2.09	4.67	10.86	91	10.27	3.45	3.25	19.45
42	6.31	2.11	4.64	11.04	92	10.35	3.48	3.22	19.62
43	6.39	2.14	4.61	11.21	93	10.43	3.50	3.20	19.79
44	6.47	2.17	4.58	11.38	94	10.51	3.53	3.18	19.96
45	6.55	2.20	4.55	11.55	95	10.59	3.56	3.15	20.14
46	6.63	2.22	4.52	11.72	96	10.67	3.59	3.12	20.31
47	6.71	2.25	4.50	11.89	97	10.75	3.61	3.09	20.48
48	6.79	2.28	4.47	12.07	98	10.83	3.64	3.06	20.65
49	6.87	2.30	4.44	12.24	99	10.91	3.67	3.03	20.82
50	6.95	2.33	4.41	12.41	100	11.00	3.70	3.01	21.00

Additional Point:

3 Jumps: 1 point for each 8cm above 11.00
SLJ: 1 point for each 3cm above 3.70

30m 1 point for each 0.03 below 3.01
OH Shot 1 point for each 7cmabove 21.00

FURTHER READING

TEACHING THE THROWS
How to Teach the Throws – C. T. Johnson (B.A.F.)
But First – F. W. Dick (B.A.F.)

TECHNIQUE
Athletes in Action – Editor H. Payne (Pelham Books)
Throwing – Max Jones (Crowood Press)
Track and Field Technique through Dynamics – Tom Ecker (Track & Field News)
The Mechanics of Athletics – G. Dyson (Hodder & Stoughton)
The Biomechanics of Sports Techniques – J. G. Hay (Prentice-Hall)

STRENGTH TRAINING
Strength Training – Max Jones (B.A.F.)
Weightlifting – John Lear (E. P. Books)
The Powerlifting Manual – John Lear (E. P. Books)
Powerlifting – A Scientific Approach – F. C. Hatfield (Contemporary Books)
Designing Resistance Training Programmes – Fleck/Kraemer (Human Kinetics)

TRAINING THEORY
Nutrition for Sport – Steve Wootton (Simon & Schuster)
The Science of Track & Field Athletics – H & R Payne (Pelham Books)
Training Theory – F. W. Dick (B.A.F.)
Assistant Club Coach – Coaching Theory Manual – (B.A.F.)
Club Coach – Coaching Theory Manual – (B.A.F.)
Senior Coach – Coaching Theory Manual – (B.A.F.)
Principles of Sports Training – (Sportverlag, G.D.R.)
Mobility Training – N. Brook (B.A.F.)
Sports Training Principles – F. W. Dick (A & C Black)
Athletic Ability and the Anatomy of Motion – R. Wirhed (Wolfe Medical Publications)

MAGAZINES
'The Thrower' – Editor Max Jones, 160 sides annually on the four throwing events – technique, sequence analysis, profiles, statistics etc. from – The Thrower, 152 Longdon Road, Knowle, Solihull B93 9HU
Athletics Coach – B.A.F. quarterly coaching journal from – B.A.F. Coaching Office, 225a Bristol Road, Birmingham B5 7UB

Myrtle Augee – A Commonwealth Champion and a nineteen metre thrower.

First published (Geoff Dyson)   1950
Second Edition (John Le Masurier) 1959
Third Edition (Ron Pickering)   1968
Fourth Edition (Carl Johnson)   1976
Fifth Edition (Max Jones)   1987
This Edition (Max Jones)   1995

ISBN 0 85134 126 8   2.5M/42.5M/02.95

© British Athletic Federation
225A Bristol Road
Birmingham B5 7UB

Typeset in Times, designed and printed on
115gsm Fineblade Cartridge in England by
Woodcote Limited, Epsom, Surrey KT18 7HL

SHOT PUTTING

Max Jones

(B.A.F. National Coach)